# All-Time Favorites for
# ACCORDION

**Arranged by Gary Meisner**

## CONTENTS

ISBN 978-0-634-07015-0

HAL•LEONARD®
CORPORATION
7777 W. BLUEMOUND RD. P.O. BOX 13819 MILWAUKEE, WI 53213

Visit Hal Leonard Online at
**www.halleonard.com**

# AIN'T MISBEHAVIN'

Words by ANDY RAZAF
Music by THOMAS "FATS" WALLER
and HARRY BROOKS

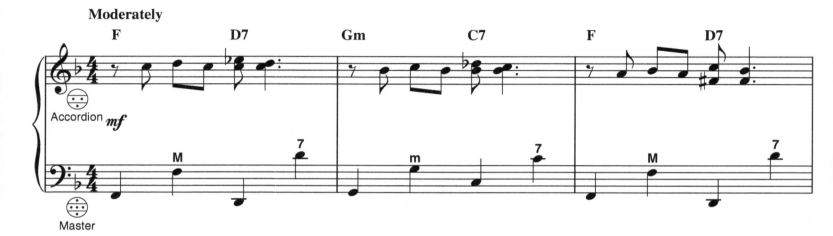

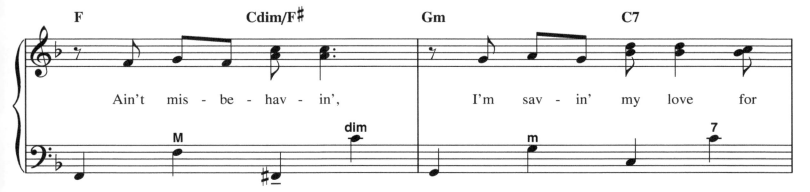

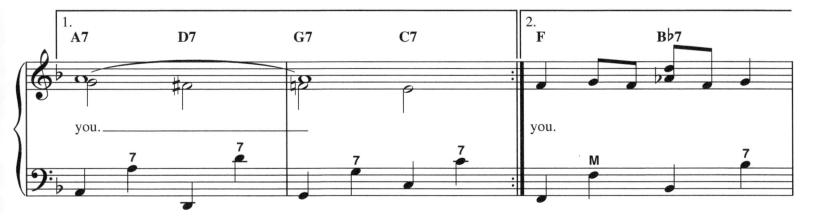

4

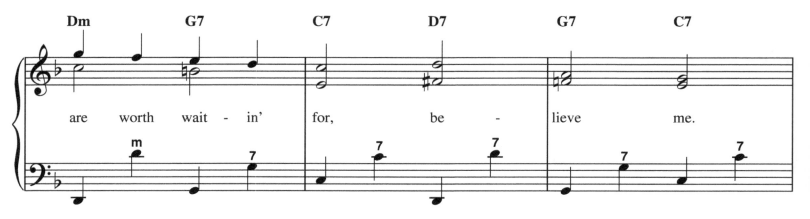

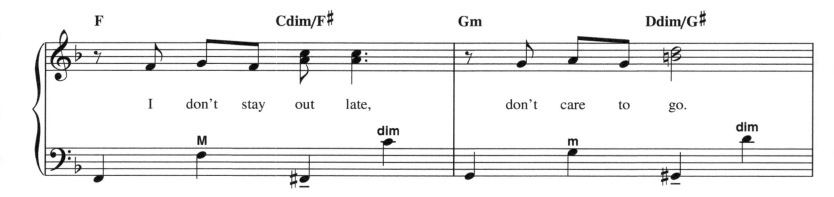

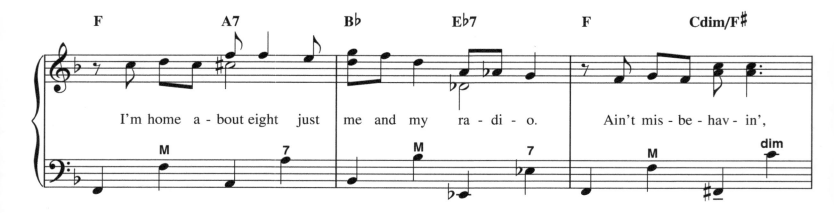

# AUTUMN LEAVES

English lyric by JOHNNY MERCER
French lyric by JACQUES PREVERT
Music by JOSEPH KOSMA

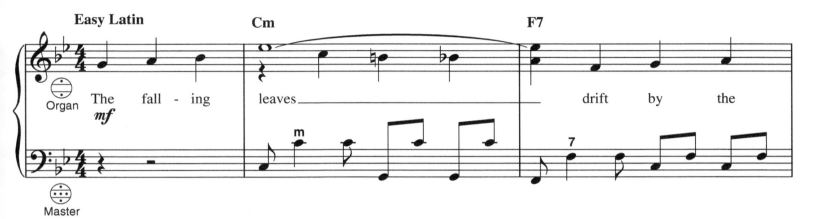

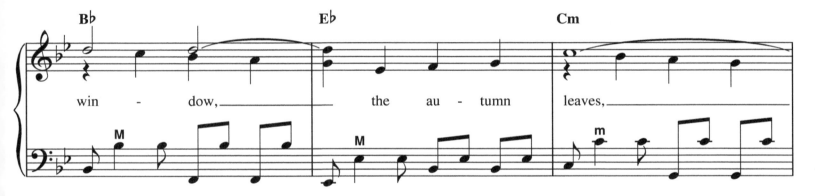

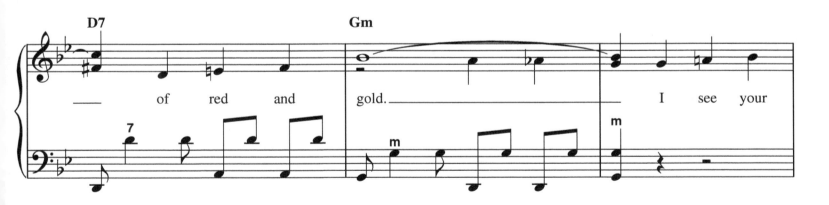

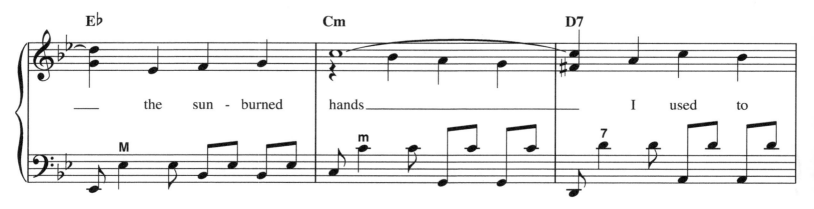

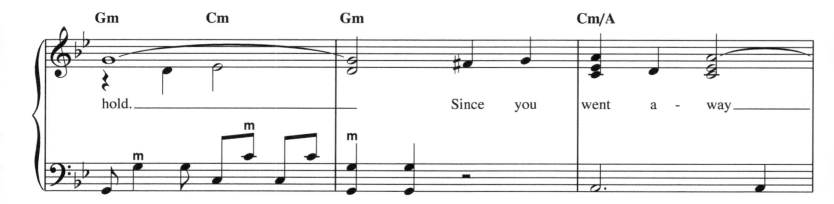

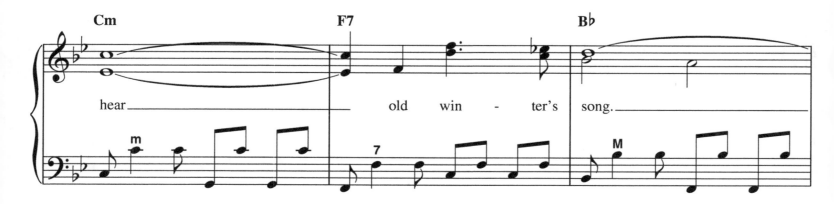

But I miss you most of all, my

dar - ling, _____ when au - tumn

leaves start to fall. _____

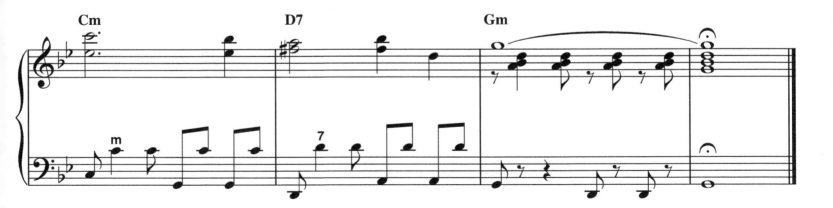

# BUBBLES IN THE WINE
### featured in the Television Series THE LAWRENCE WELK SHOW

Words and Music by FRANK LOESSER,
BOB CALAME and LAWRENCE WELK

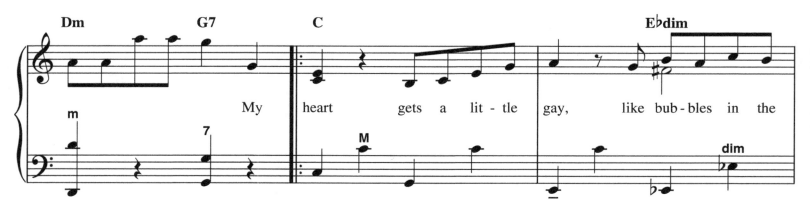

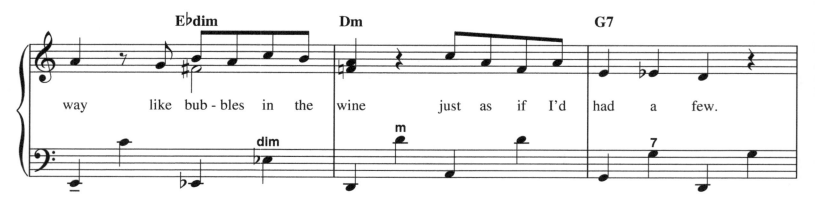

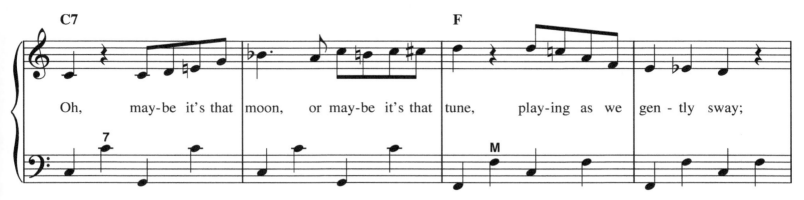

Oh, may-be it's that moon, or may-be it's that tune, play-ing as we gen-tly sway;

or may - be it's the fact that I love you. Can't real - ly say, how I

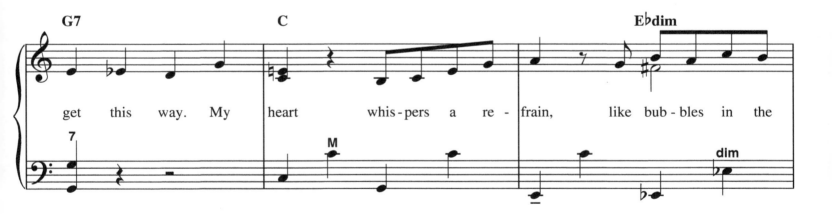

get this way. My heart whis-pers a re - frain, like bub - bles in the

wine ev - 'ry time you're close to me. I need - n't drink cham -

pagne, a feel-ing quite in - sane lights me up and sets me free. Some day I may lose you, but no

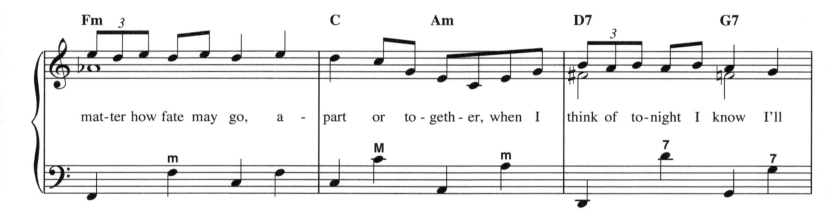

mat-ter how fate may go, a - part or to - geth - er, when I think of to-night I know I'll

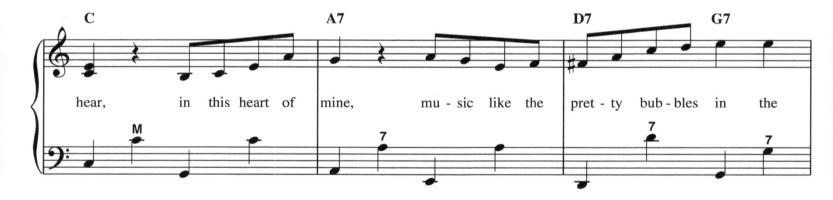

hear, in this heart of mine, mu - sic like the pret - ty bub - bles in the

wine.    wine.

# THE CANDY MAN

## from WILLY WONKA AND THE CHOCOLATE FACTORY

Words and Music by LESLIE BRICUSSE
and ANTHONY NEWLEY

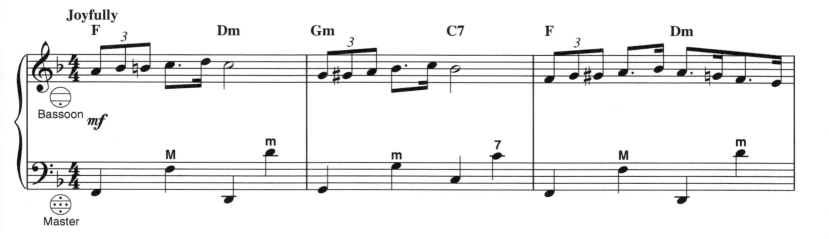

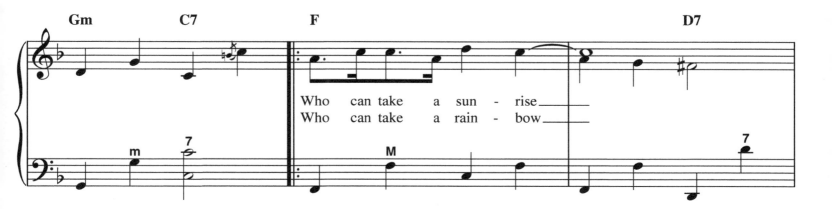

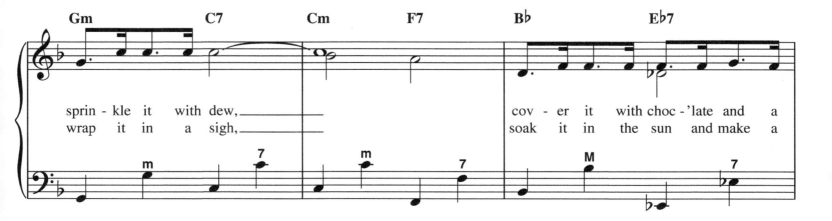

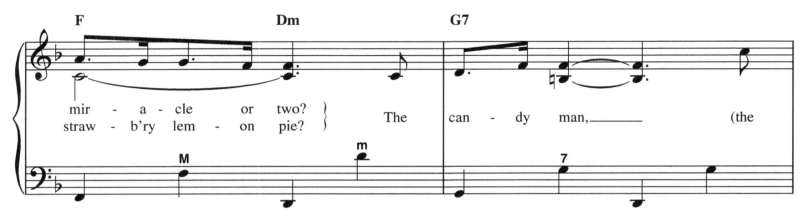

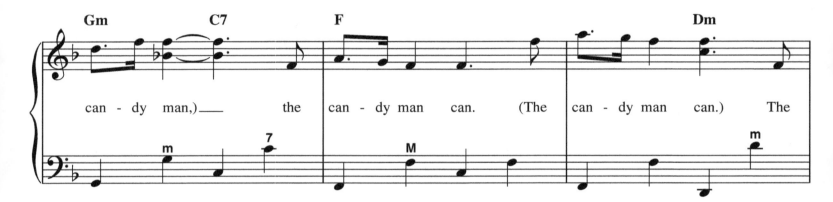

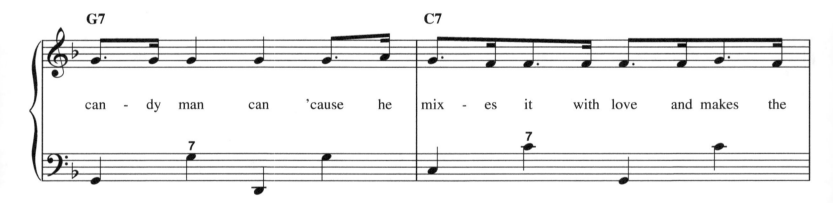

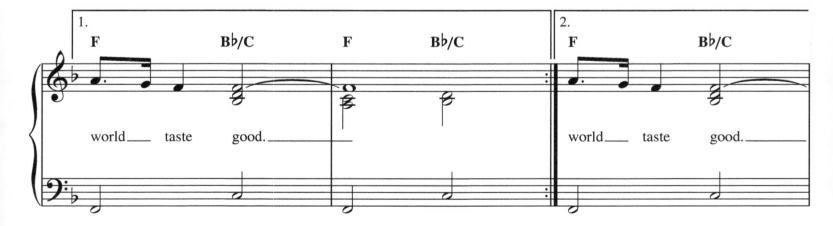

The can - dy man makes ev - 'ry-thing he bakes

sat - is - fy - ing and de - li - cious.

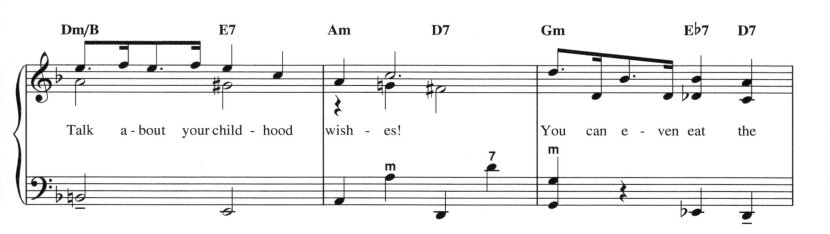

Talk a - bout your child - hood wish - es! You can e - ven eat the

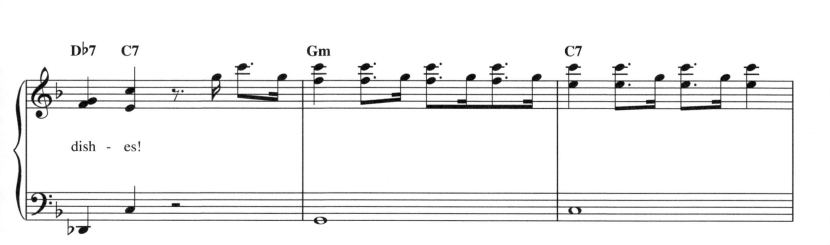

dish - es!

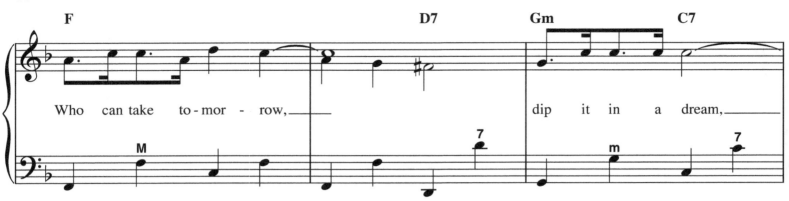

Who can take to-mor - row,_____ dip it in a dream,_____

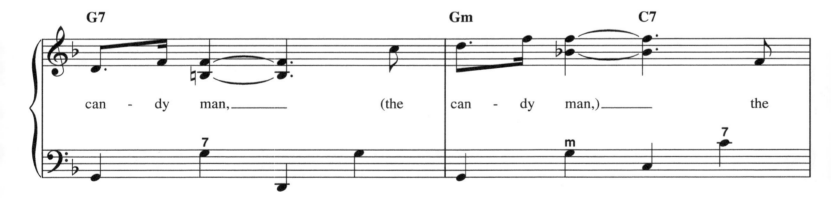

_____ sep - a - rate the sor - row and col - lect up all the cream? The

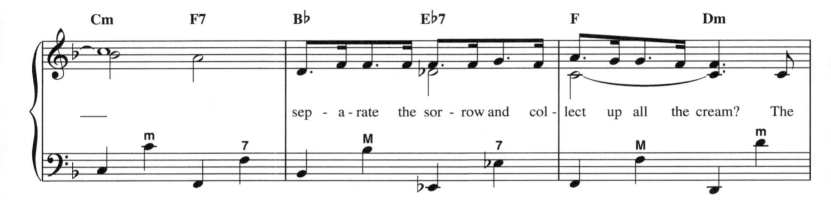

can - dy man,_____ (the can - dy man,)_____ the

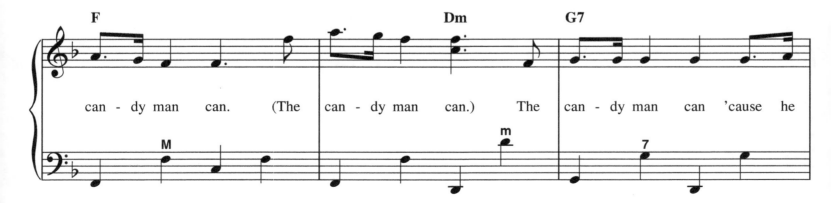

can - dy man can. (The can - dy man can.) The can - dy man can 'cause he

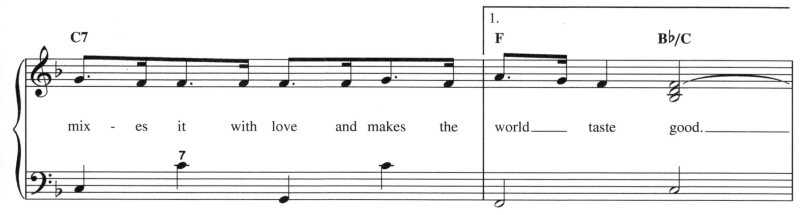

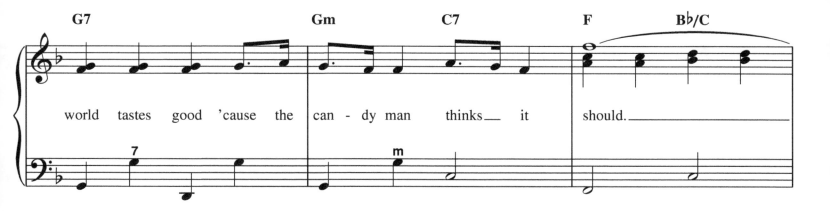

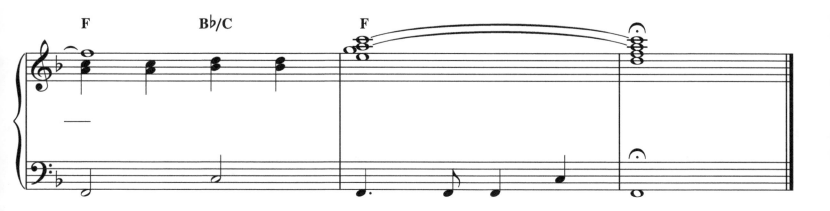

# CRAZY

Words and Music by
WILLIE NELSON

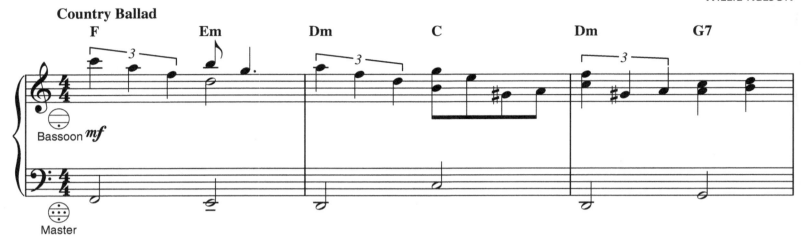

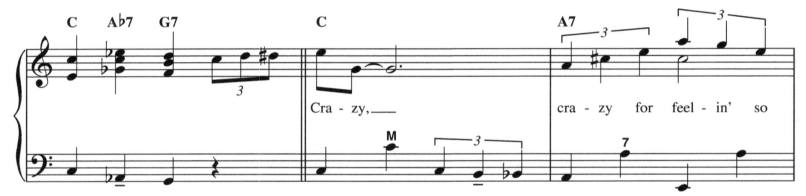

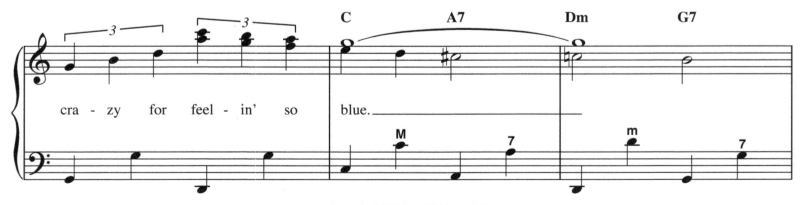

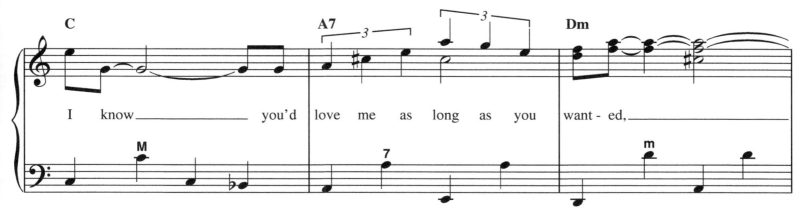

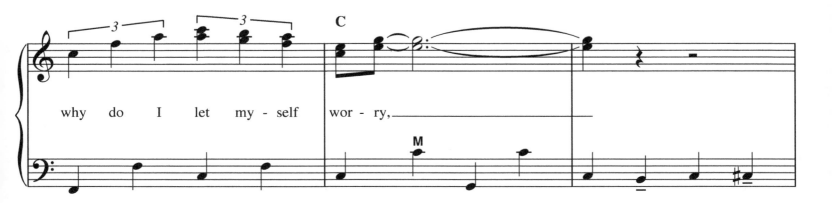

won - d'rin' __ what in the world did I do?

Cra - zy _____ for think - ing that my love could

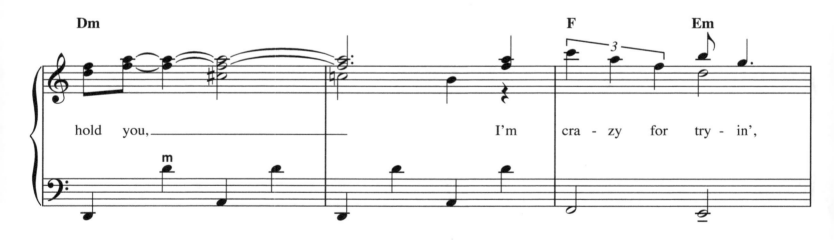

hold you, _____ I'm cra - zy for try - in',

cra - zy for cry - in' and I'm cra - zy for lov - in' you!

# FLY ME TO THE MOON
## (In Other Words)

Words and Music by
BART HOWARD

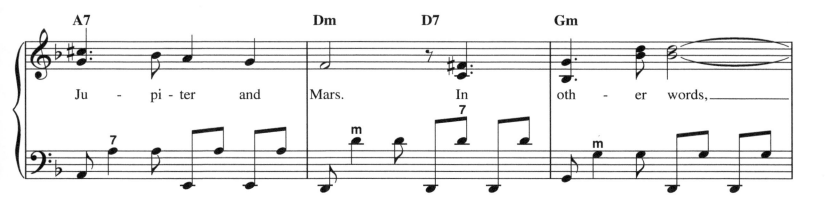

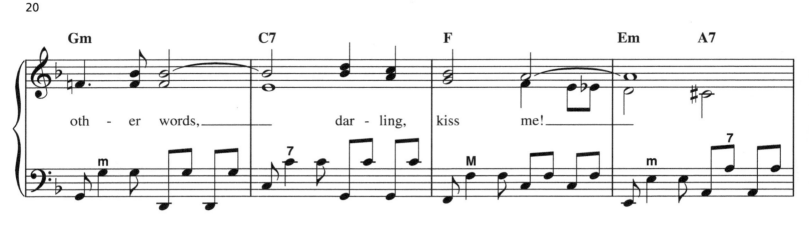

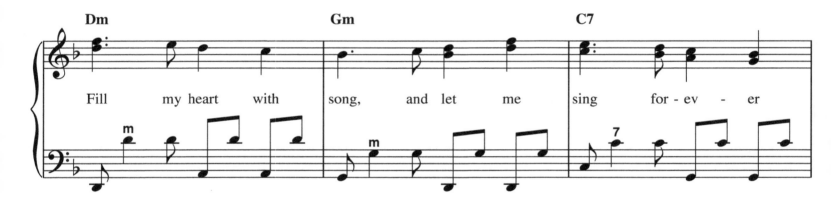

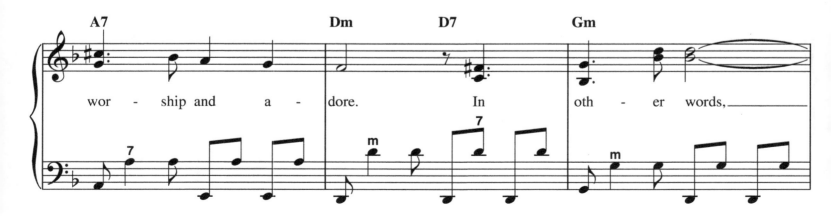

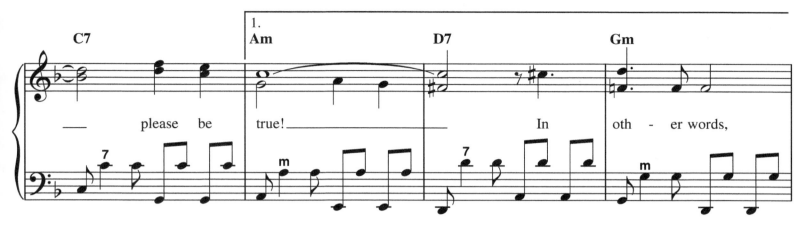

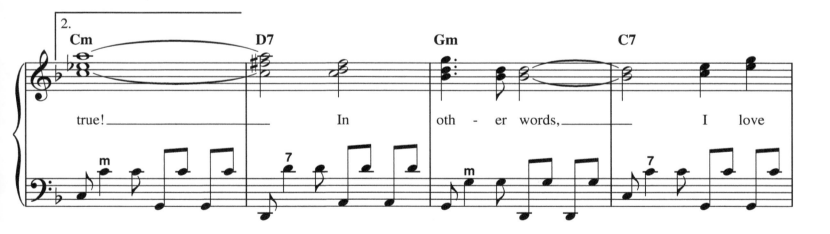

# HELLO, DOLLY!

Music and Lyric by
JERRY HERMAN

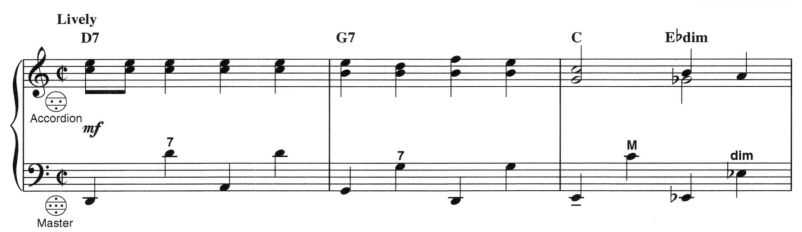

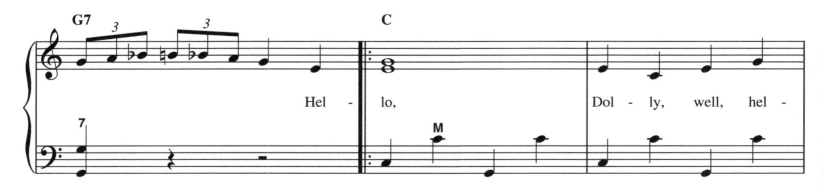

Hel - lo, Dol - ly, well, hel -

lo, Dol - ly, it's so nice to have you back where you be -

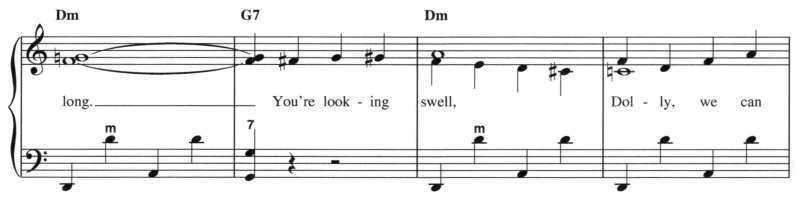

long._____ You're look - ing swell, Dol - ly, we can

tell, Dol - ly, you're still glow - in', you're still crow - in', you're still

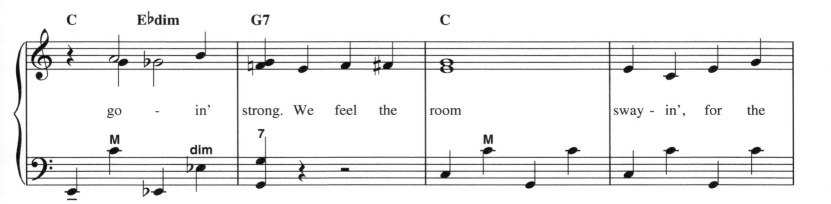

go - in' strong. We feel the room sway - in', for the

band's play - in' one of your old fa - v'rite songs from 'way back

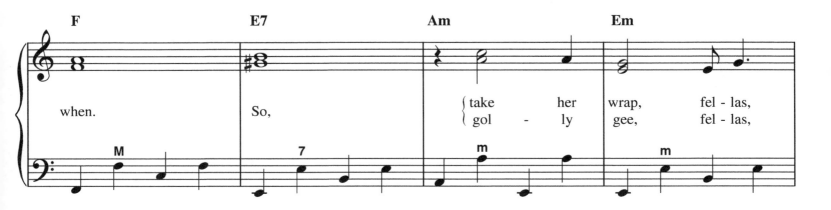

when. So, { take her wrap, fel - las, { gol - ly gee, fel - las,

find her an emp - ty lap, fel - las.)
find her a va - cant knee, fel - las.)
Dol - ly 'll nev - er

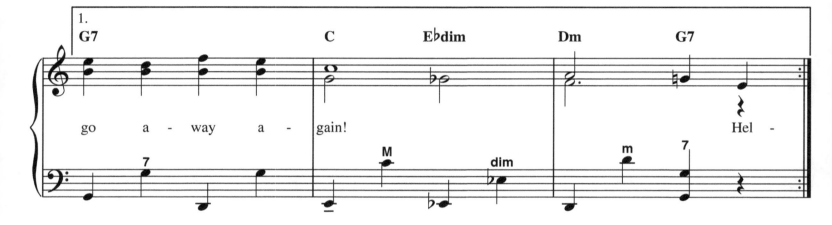

go a - way a - gain!
Hel -

go a - way,
Dol - ly 'll nev - er go a - way,

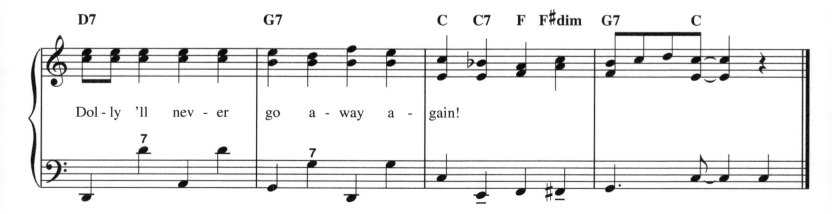

Dol - ly 'll nev - er go a - way a - gain!

# I LOVE PARIS

**from CAN-CAN**
**from HIGH SOCIETY**

Words and Music by
COLE PORTER

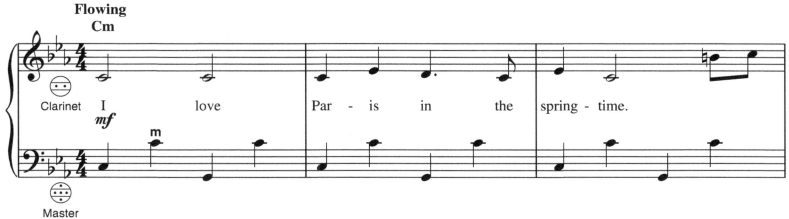

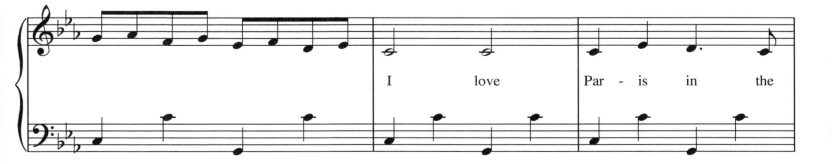

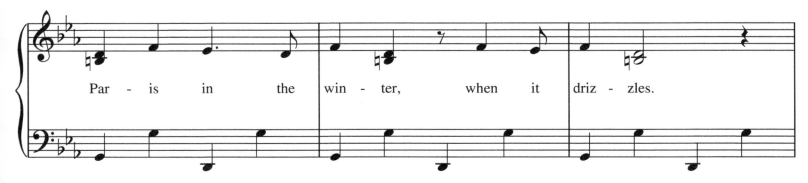

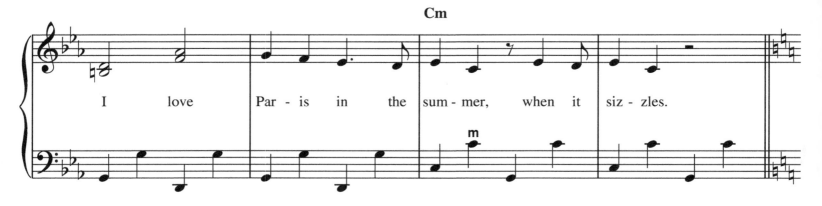

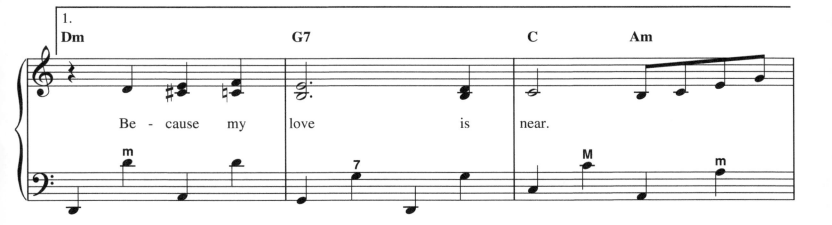

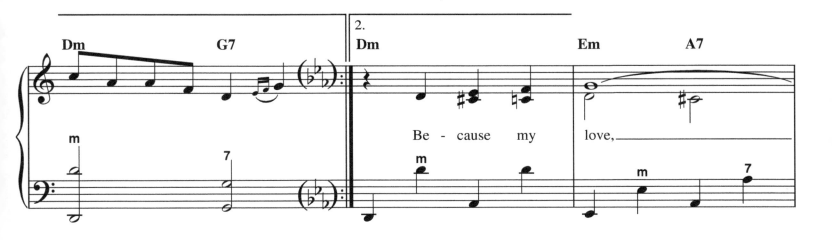

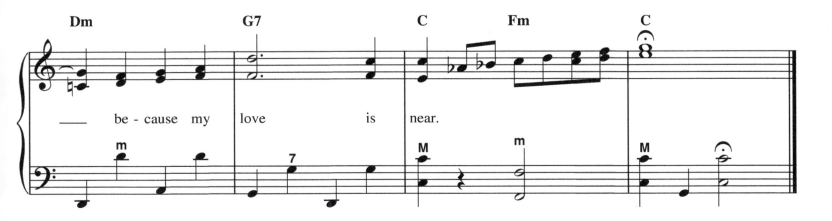

# HEY, GOOD LOOKIN'

Words and Music by
HANK WILLIAMS

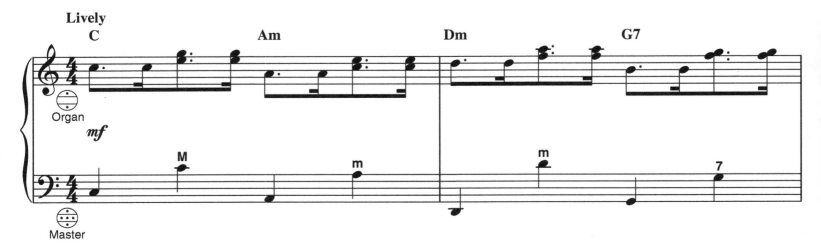

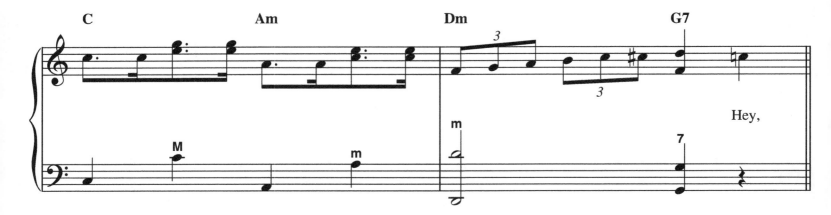

Hey,

hey,        good    look- in',           what - cha got
free        and    read- y,     so        we    can go

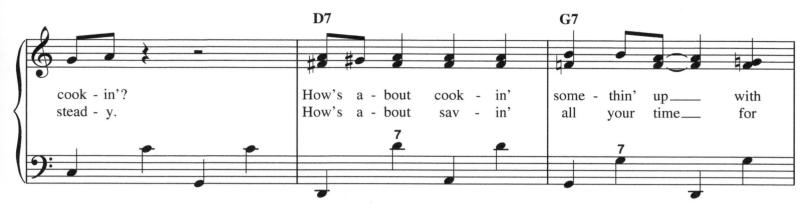

cook - in'?
stead - y.

How's a - bout cook - in'
How's a - bout sav - in'

some - thin' up_____ with
all your time_____ for

me?
me?

Hey,
No

sweet
more

ba - by,
look - in',

I

don't_____ you think
know_____ I've been

may - be
took - en

we could find us a
how's a - bout keep - in'

brand - new rec - i -
stead - y com - pa -

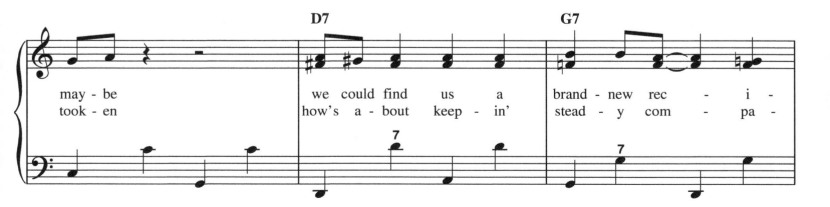

30

what - cha got cook - in'? How's a - bout cook - in'

some - thin' up_____ with me? I'm
some - thin' up_____ with,

how's a - bout cook - in' some - thin' up_____ with, how's a - bout cook - in'

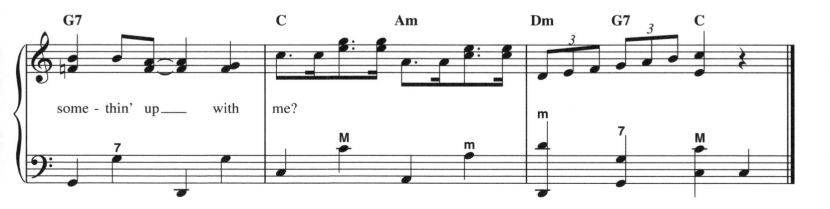

some - thin' up_____ with me?

# I'VE GROWN ACCUSTOMED TO HER FACE

from MY FAIR LADY

Words by ALAN JAY LERNER
Music by FREDERICK LOEWE

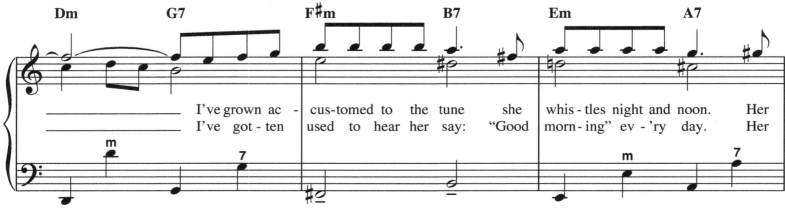

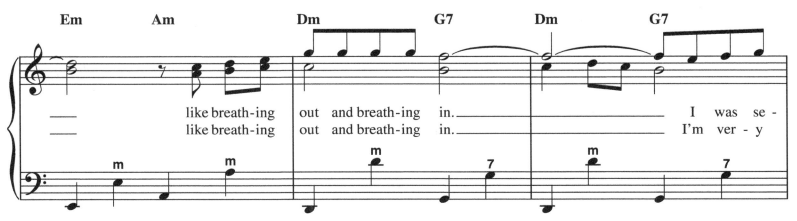

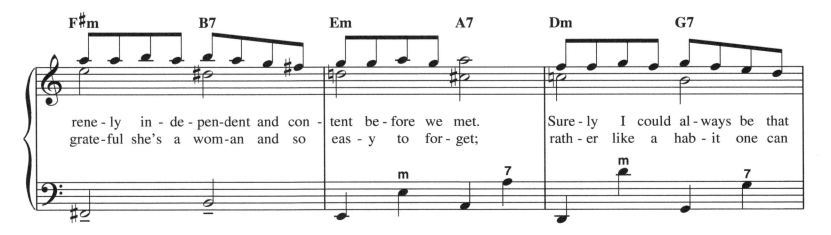

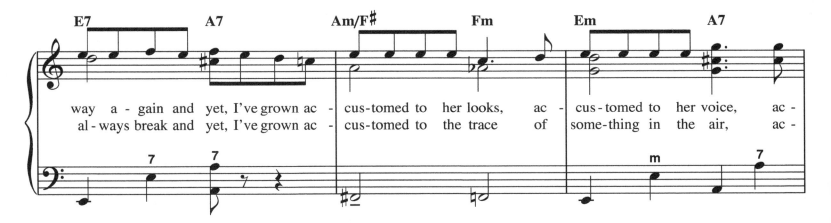

# MOON RIVER
## from the Paramount Picture BREAKFAST AT TIFFANY'S

Words by JOHNNY MERCER
Music by HENRY MANCINI

**Slowly**

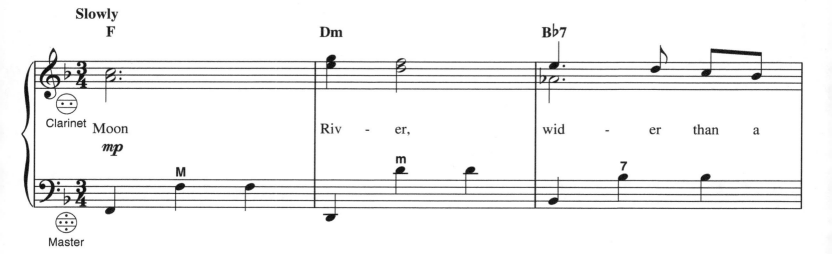

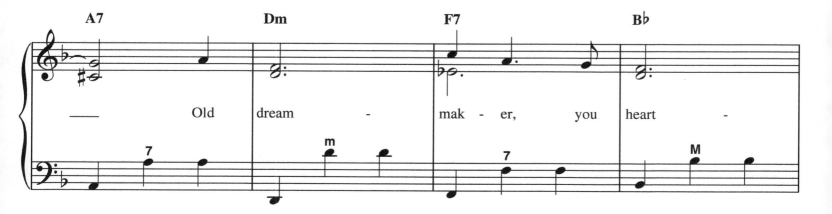

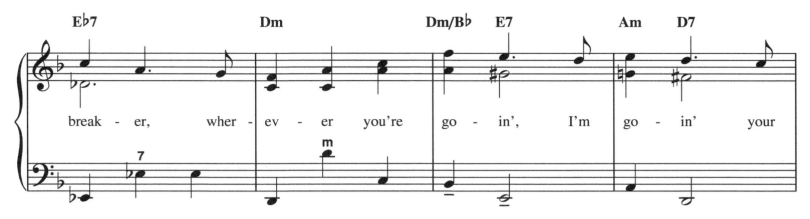

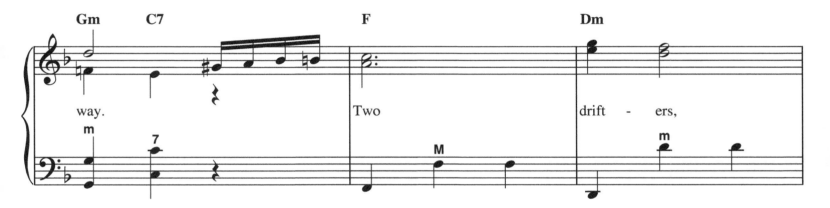

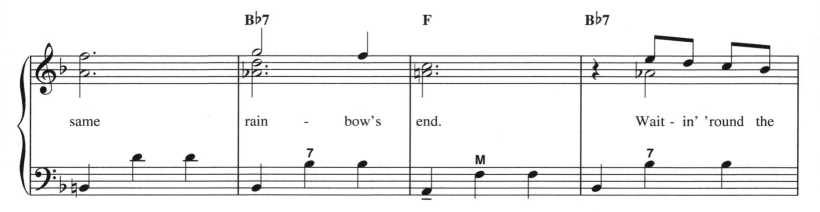

same                    rain - bow's        end.                    Wait - in' 'round the

bend,                              my  Huck - le - ber - ry        friend,

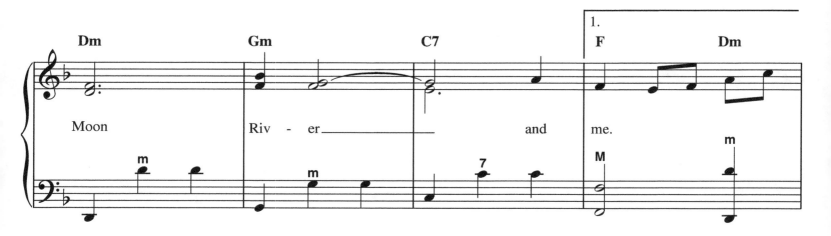

Moon                    Riv - er_____                    and   me.

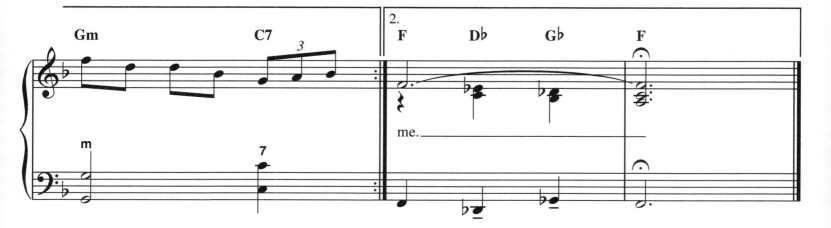

me._____

# MY CHERIE AMOUR

Words and Music by STEVIE WONDER,
SYLVIA MOY and HENRY COSBY

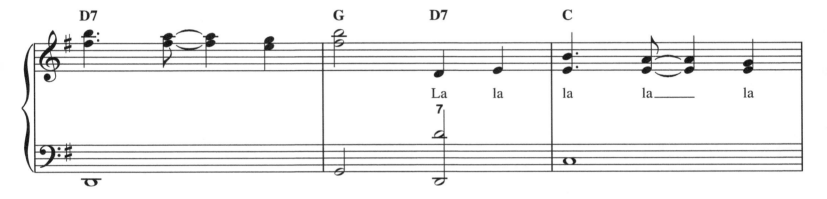

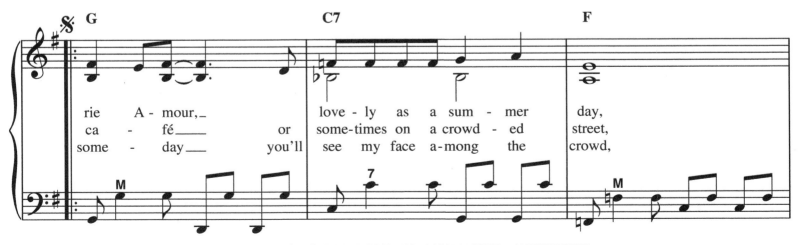

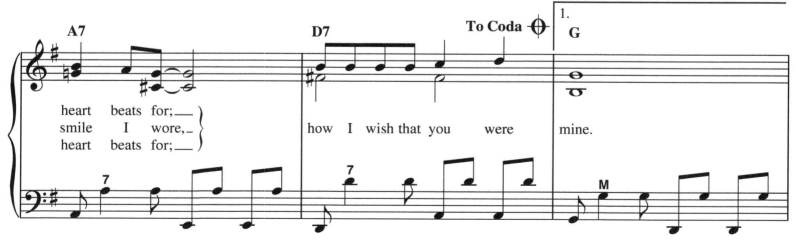

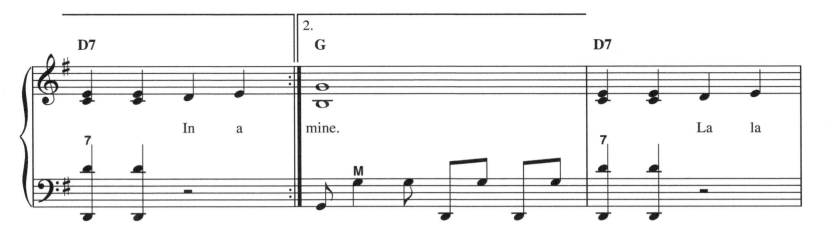

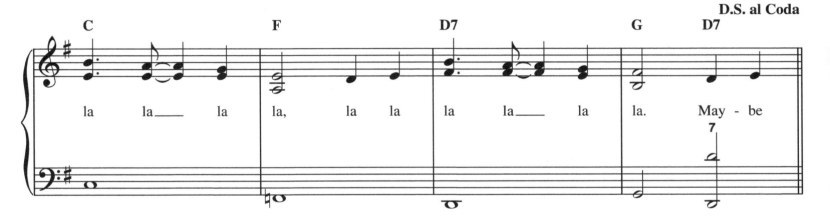

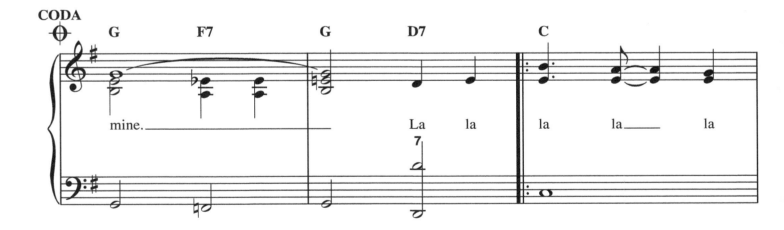

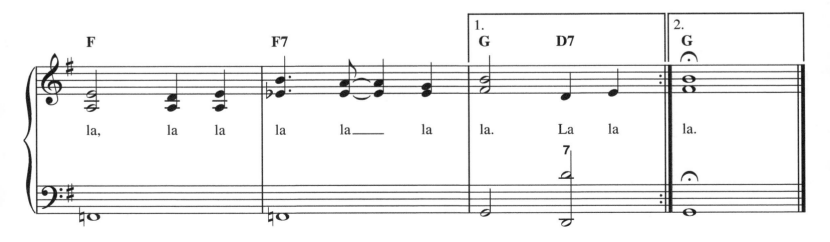

# MY WAY

English Words by PAUL ANKA
Original French Words by GILLES THIBAULT
Music by JACQUES REVAUX and CLAUDE FRANCOIS

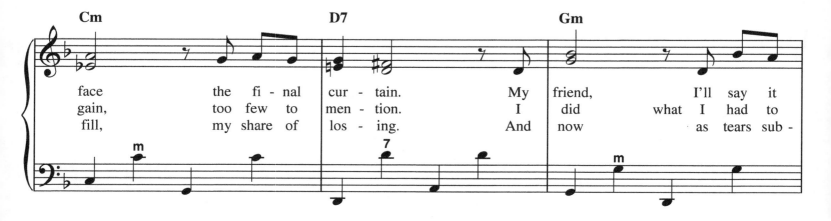

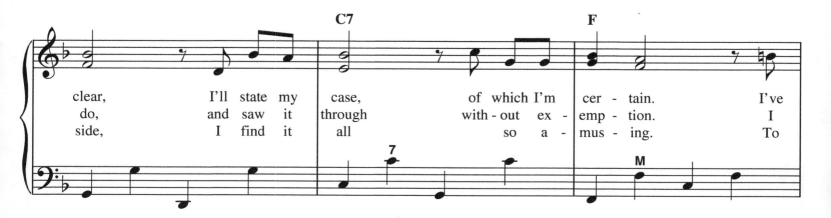

41

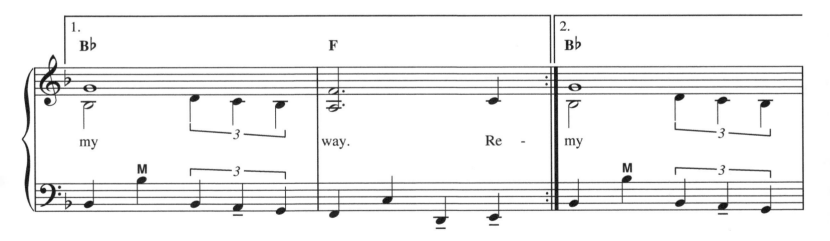

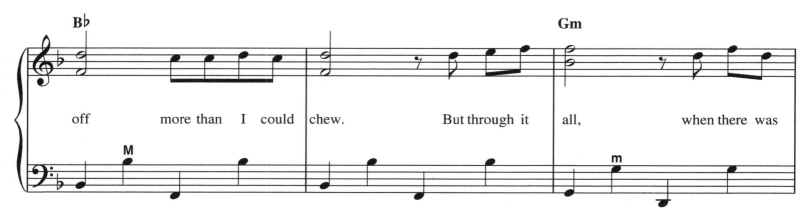

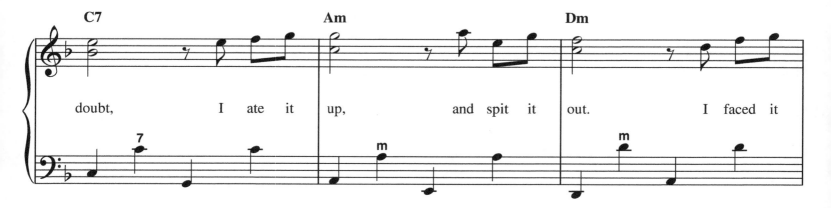

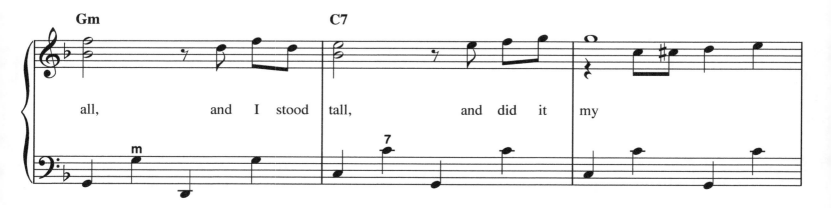

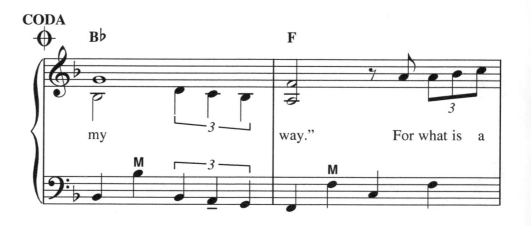

man, what has he got? If not him - self, then he has

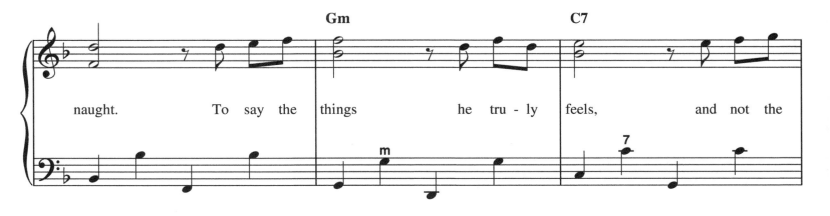

naught. To say the things he tru - ly feels, and not the

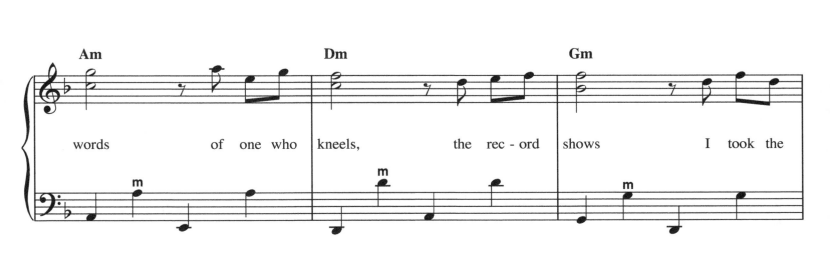

words of one who kneels, the rec - ord shows I took the

blows, and did it my way.

# SLOW POKE

Words and Music by PEE WEE KING,
REDD STEWART and CHILTON PRICE

© 1951 (Renewed 1979) Ridgeway Music Co., Inc.
All Rights Reserved   Used by Permission

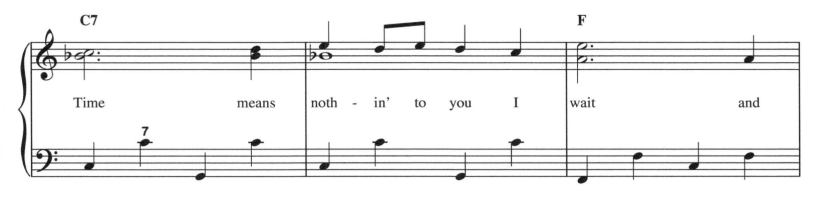

Time means noth - in' to you I wait and

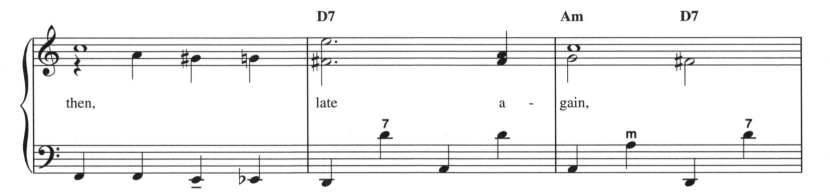

then, late a - gain,

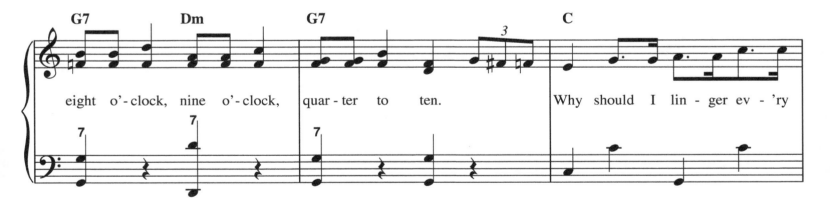

eight o'- clock, nine o'- clock, quar - ter to ten. Why should I lin - ger ev - 'ry

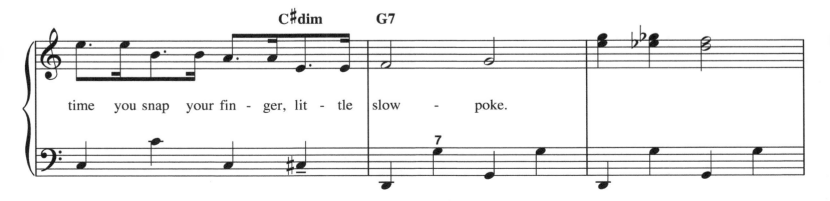

time you snap your fin - ger, lit - tle slow - poke.

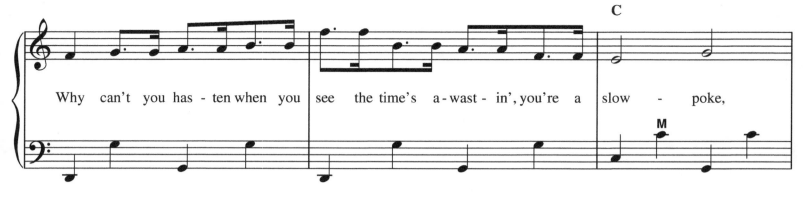

Why can't you has-ten when you see the time's a-wast-in', you're a slow - poke,

dear. Why should I keep try-in' to change you,

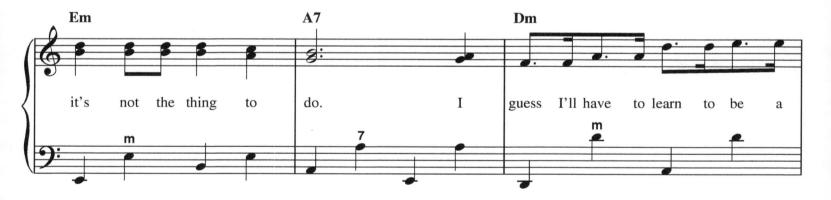

it's not the thing to do. I guess I'll have to learn to be a

slow - poke too!

# SPEAK SOFTLY, LOVE
## (Love Theme)
### from the Paramount Picture THE GODFATHER

Words by LARRY KUSIK
Music by NINO ROTA

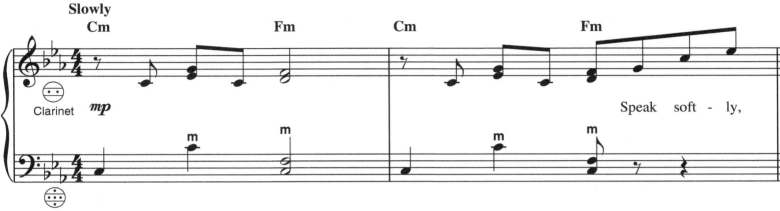

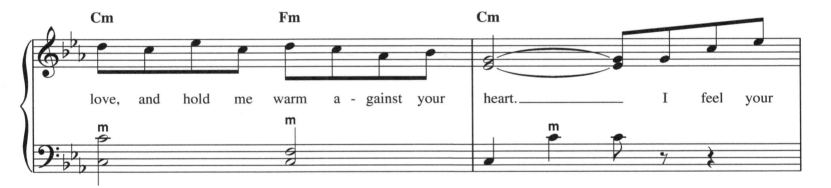

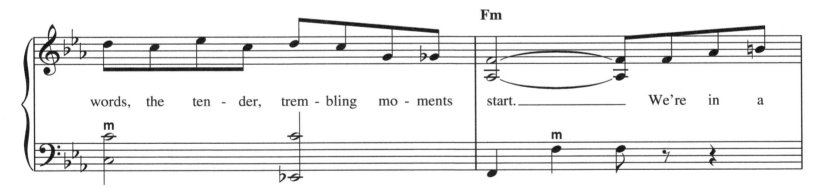

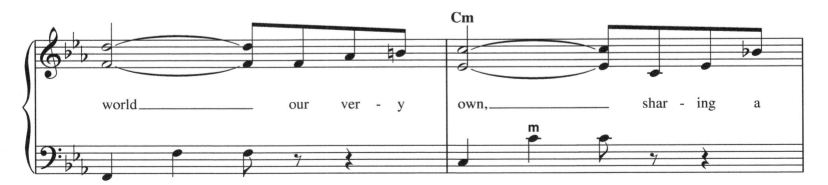

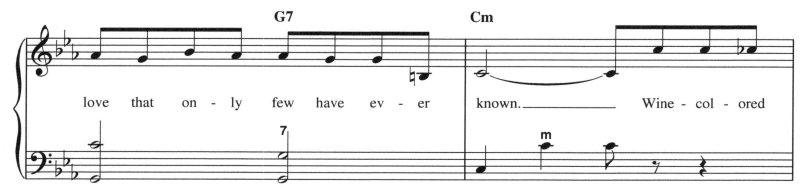

love that on - ly few have ev - er known._____ Wine - col - ored

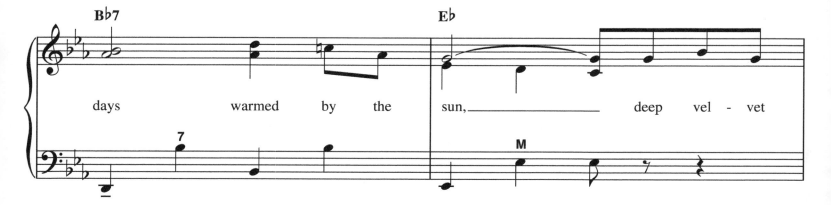

days warmed by the sun,_____ deep vel - vet

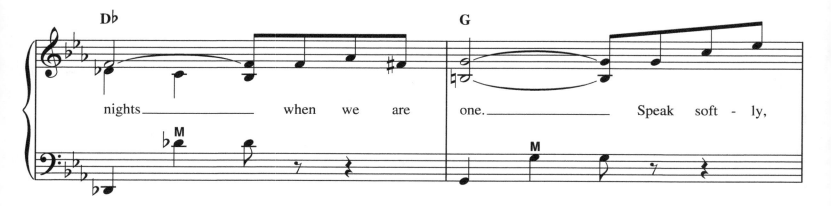

nights_____ when we are one._____ Speak soft - ly,

love, so no one hears us but the sky._____ The vows of

love we make will live un - til we die._____ My life is

yours_____ and all be - cause_____ you came in -

to my world with love so soft - ly, love.

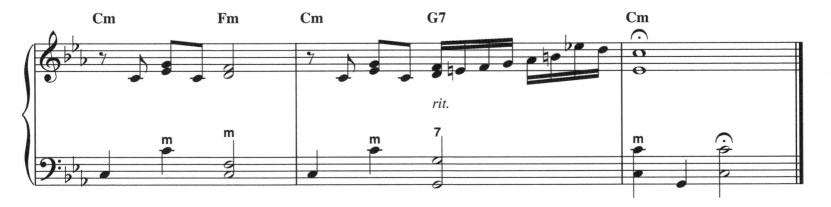

# SPEAK LOW
## from the Musical Production ONE TOUCH OF VENUS

Words by OGDEN NASH
Music by KURT WEILL

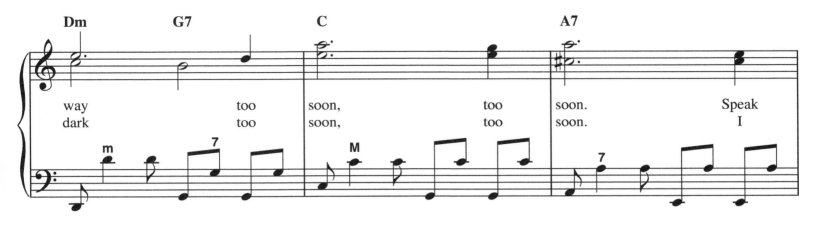

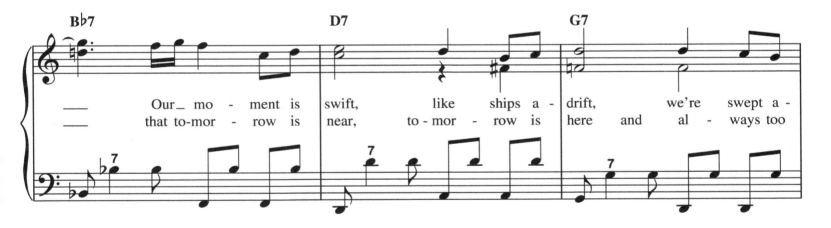

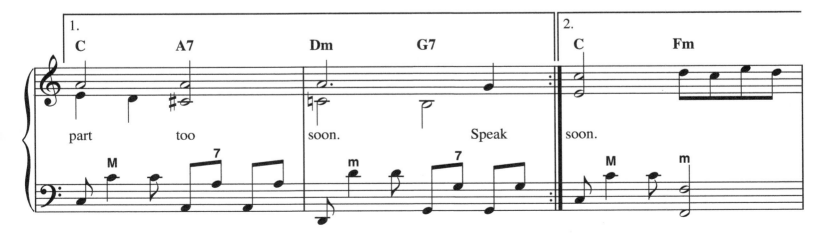

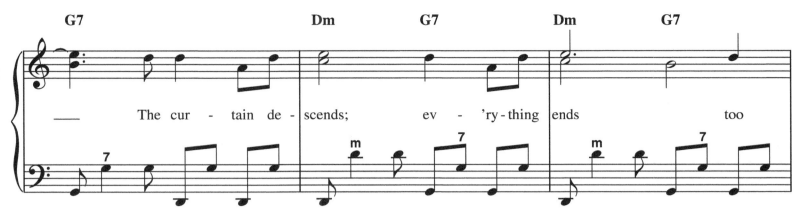

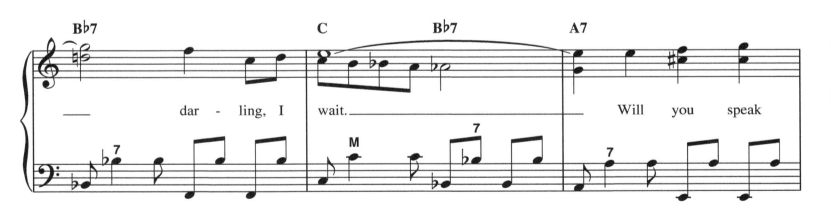

# UNCHAINED MELODY

### from the Motion Picture UNCHAINED

Lyric by HY ZARET
Music by ALEX NORTH

Oh, my love, my dar - ling, I've hun - gered for your

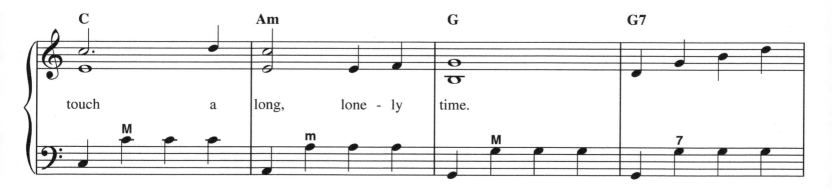

touch a long, lone - ly time.

Time goes by so slow - ly and time can do so

55

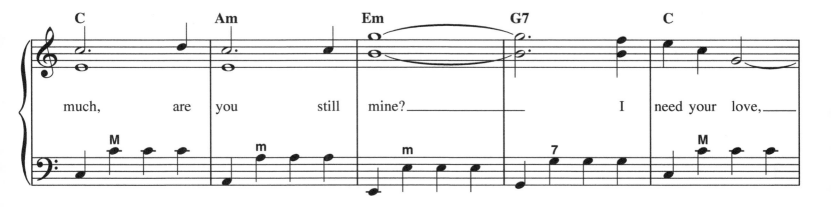

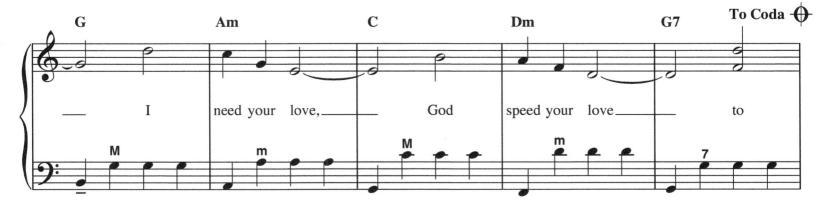

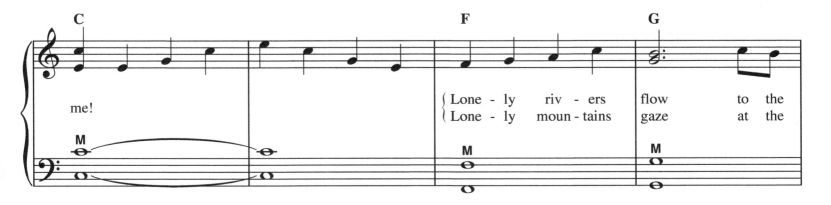

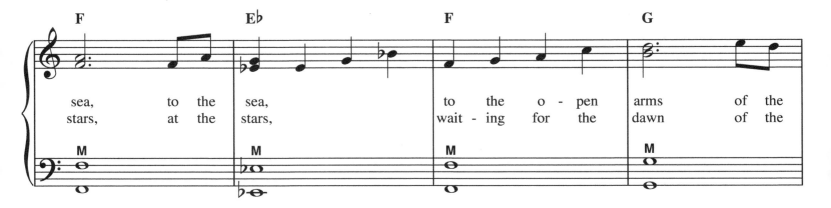

56

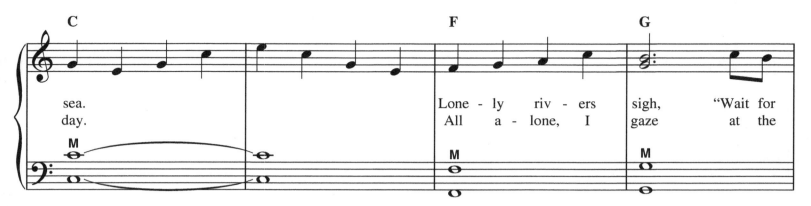

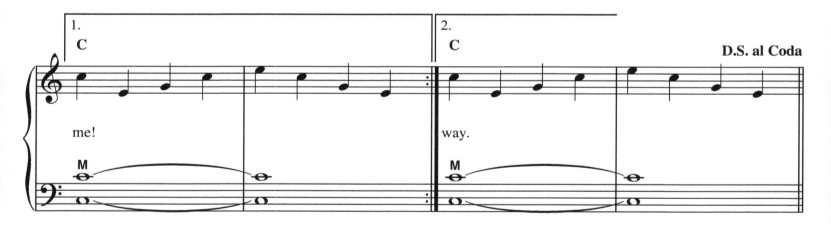

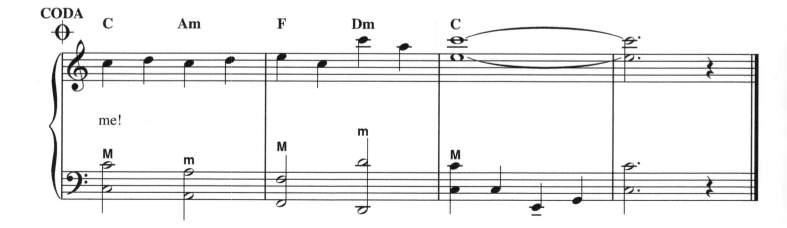

# THE WAY WE WERE

Words by ALAN and MARILYN BERGMAN
Music by MARVIN HAMLISCH

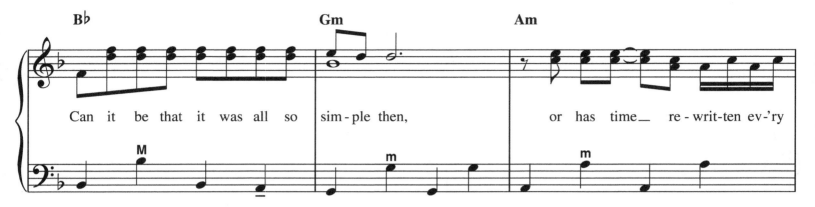

Can it be that it was all so sim-ple then, or has time re-writ-ten ev-'ry

line? If we had the chance to do it all a-gain, tell me

would we?_____ Could we?_____ Mem - 'ries_____

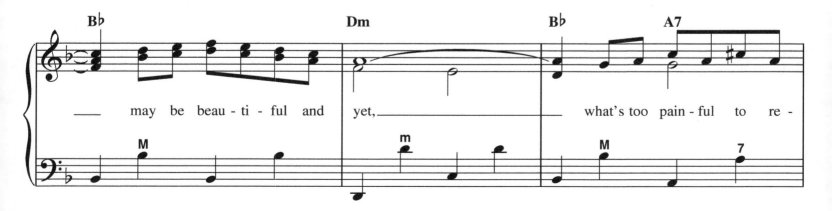

_____ may be beau-ti-ful and yet,_____ what's too pain-ful to re-

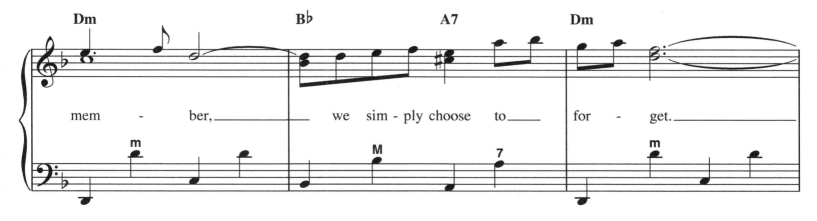

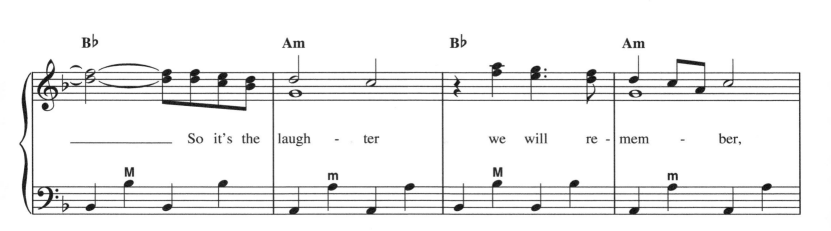

# WONDERFUL COPENHAGEN

## from the Motion Picture HANS CHRISTIAN ANDERSEN

By FRANK LOESSER

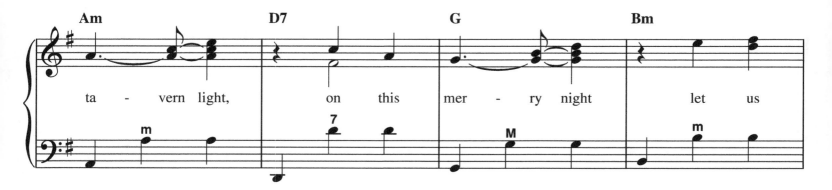

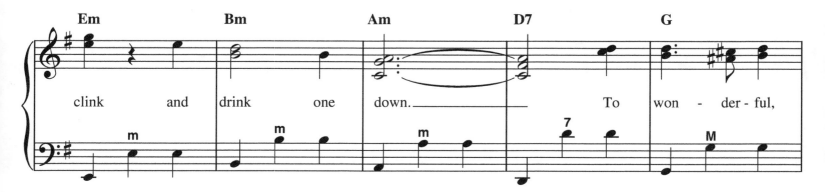

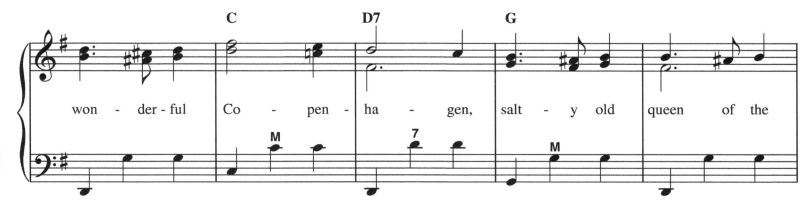

won - der - ful Co - pen - ha - gen, salt - y old queen of the

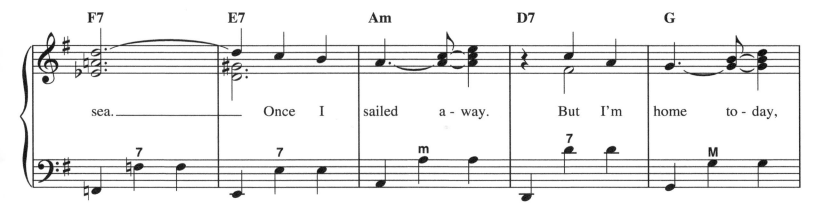

sea._____ Once I sailed a - way. But I'm home to - day,

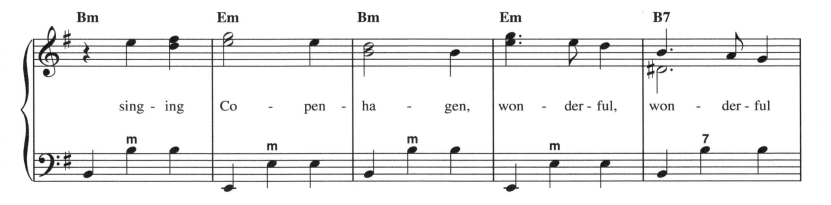

sing - ing Co - pen - ha - gen, won - der - ful, won - der - ful

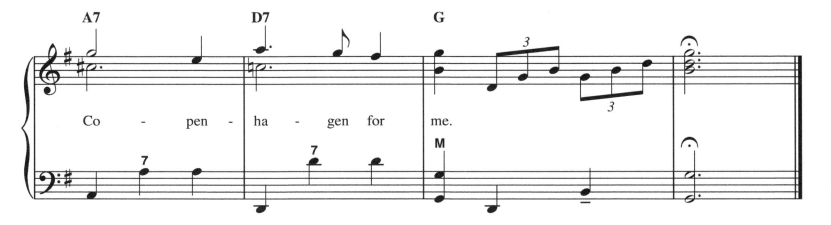

Co - pen - ha - gen for me.

# ZIP-A-DEE-DOO-DAH

from Walt Disney's SONG OF THE SOUTH
from Disneyland and Walt Disney World's SPLASH MOUNTAIN

Words by RAY GILBERT
Music by ALLIE WRUBEL

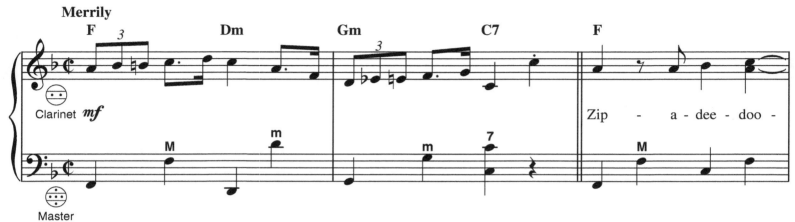

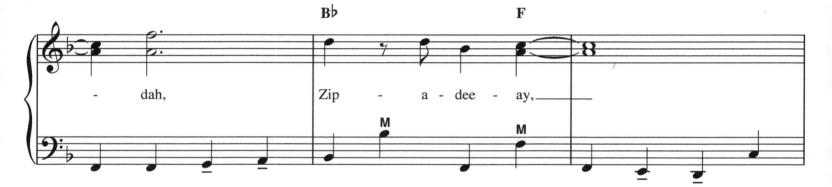

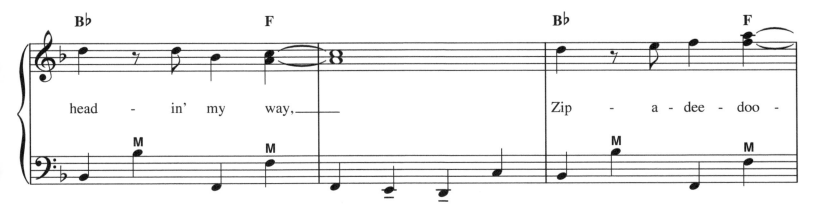

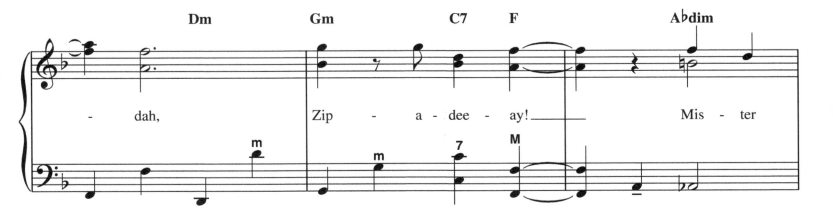

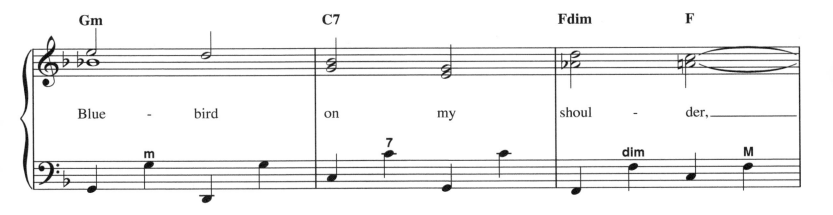

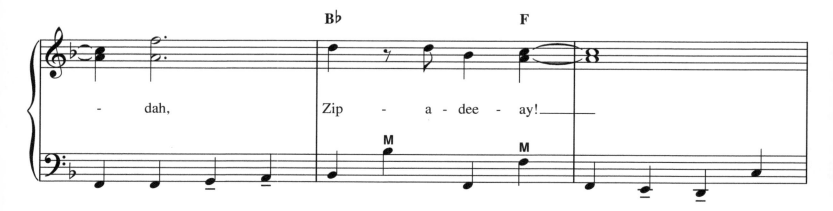

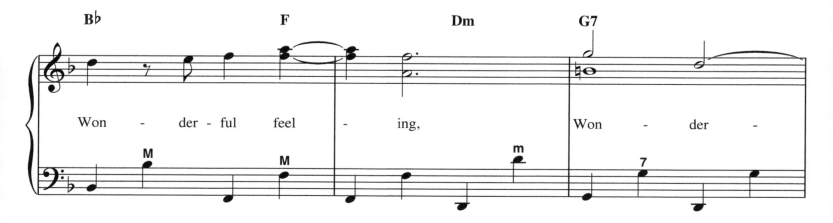

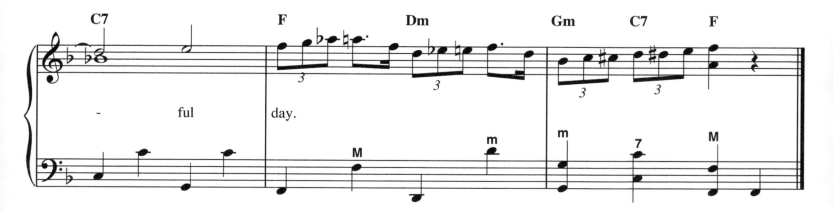